The Laughing Calvinist

The Laughing Calvinist

Poems by

Christina E. Petrides

© 2025 Christina E. Petrides. All rights reserved.
This material may not be reproduced in any form, published,
reprinted, recorded, performed, broadcast,
rewritten or redistributed without
the explicit permission of Christina E. Petrides.
All such actions are strictly prohibited by law.

Cover image by Chris Curry on Unsplash
Author photo by Karen Jones

ISBN: 978-1-63980-800-7

Kelsay Books
502 South 1040 East, A-119
American Fork, Utah 84003
Kelsaybooks.com

To Tammy (신선옥),
for her cheerful friendship
and for the poetic inspiration she always provides.

Acknowledgments

Grateful acknowledgment is made to the editors of these journals and chapbooks where the following poems appeared, some in earlier versions.

2022

2023 Texas Poetry Calendar (Kallisto Gaia, 2023): "Academy"
Active Muse: "Medusa," "Irish Seahorses"
Black Fox Literary Magazine: "Fall"
Christmas Cheerios (Wingless Dreamer, 2023): "Advent Sweets"
Clepsydra Literary and Art Magazine: "Inspiring Circumstances"
Coffin Bell Journal: "February 13, 2021"
Fresh Words Magazine: "Mortal Dread," "Urban Late Summer"
The Flying Dodo: "Fall/Winter"
In the Garden (Torrey House: 2022): "Garden Stitchery"
isotrope: "Restless Spirit"
LitBop: "Eve" and "Missing"
Meow Meow Pow Pow Lit: "Volcano"
My Unheard September (Wingless Dreamer, 2022): "Junior High"
Open Minds Quarterly: "To Rest"
Sequoia Speaks: "Before, Then, After," "2022," "Haunted," "Ideal," "Words II"
Taj Mahal Review: "Mature Chemistry"
Unbound Brooklyn Journal: "Late Love," "Fissures"
Valiant Scribe Literary Journal: "Insomnia," "Theological Tanka"
Vita Poetica Journal: "Respite"
Wilderness House Literary Review: "Saving and Spending," "Tampa Tanka," "Fear"
The Writing Disorder: "Contemplating Autobiography," "Poetry," "Seogwipo Weekday, 3 PM"

2023

Bear Creek Gazette: "Philosophical"
Cosmic Daffodil Journal: "Recompense"
Dipity Literary Magazine: "Antique Music"
Gastopoda: "Autumn Walk"
Home Planet News: "Reclaimed," "Wanderer's Dilemma," "Be Nimble"
The Legend: "Bodega"
OpenDoor Magazine: "Unmatched"
Perceptions Magazine: "Jungang Rotary on Buddha's Birthday"
Steam Ticket: "Cold"
The Scop: "Undetermined" "Fashion Show"
Switchgrass Review: "Ode to 'The Change'," "Fungus Haiku," "Boobs Haiku"

2024

The Cawnpore Magazine: "Sacrifices," "Wrinkles" "Veteran"
Cicada Creative Magazine: "Outdated"
Contemplit Magazine: "Ocean Tanka"
Haunted Portal Magazine: "Player," "Treasure," "Good Sleep"
Ranger: "Gym Notice," "Publisher's Lunch," "Conspiracy Theorists," "Weekdays," "Search Fail," "Dixie Barista"
Salvation South: "Georgia"
The Scop: "Holiday Solitude," "Tiger Food"
Star 82 Review: "Monsoon Season," "Medieval Calligraphy"

2025
7th-Circle Pyrite: "A Southern Psalm"
Active Muse: "Twilight" and "Cyclist"
Amethyst Review: "Spirit"
The Brussels Review: "Showoffs"
Journal of Expressive Writing: "Questions"
Last Leaves Magazine: "Smelly Feat"
Merion West: "Observance, 2022"
Prosetrics Magazine: "Deep Winter, 2020 Korea"
Scribeworth Magazine: "South/North, Winter 2025"

Contents

Inspiring Circumstances	15
The Laughing Calvinist	16
Poetry	17
Smelly Feat	18
Spirit	19
Words II	20
Publisher's Lunch	21
Contemplating Autobiography	22
Restless Spirit	23
Insomnia	24
To Rest	25
Good Sleep	26
Theological Tanka	27
Academy	28
ESOL	29
Pencils	30
Junior High	31
Respite	32
Seogwipo Weekday, 3 PM	33
Garden Stitchery	34
Volcano	35
Fissures	36
Deep Winter, 2020, Korea	37
South/North, Winter 2025	38
Advent Sweets	39
Jolly	40
Wanderer's Dilemma	41
Tampa Tanka	42
Urban Late Summer	43
Storm Coming	44
Monsoon Season	45
Fall	46
Autumn Walk	47

Fall/Winter	48
Bodega	49
Economy Class	50
Eve	51
Magdalene	52
Missing	53
Ocean Tanka	54
Showoffs	55
Fashion Show	56
Irish Seahorses	57
Medieval Calligraphy	58
Cyclist	59
Deserving	60
Covid	61
2022	62
2020s	63
Fear	64
Castration/Consumption	65
Philosophical	66
Georgia	67
Dixie Barista	68
A Southern Psalm	69
Antique Music	70
Saving and Spending	71
Fungus Haiku	72
Gym Notice	73
Size of Resignation	74
Ode to 'The Change'	75
Boobs Haiku	76
Unmatched	77
Beverages	78
Cold	79
Holiday Solitude	80

Jungang Rotary on Buddha's Birthday	81
Tiger Food	82
Observance, 2022	83
Weekdays	84
Conspiracy Theorists	85
Treasure	86
Be Nimble	87
Search Fail	88
Player	89
Mortal Dread	90
Sacrifices	91
Wrinkles	92
Recompense	93
Veteran	94
Sideswipe	95
Haunted	96
Before, Then, After	97
February 13, 2021	98
Questions	99
Ideal	101
Outdated	102
Once	103
Medusa	104
Twilight	105
Mature Chemistry	106
Visit	107
Reclaimed	108
Undetermined	109
Late Love	110

Inspiring Circumstances

Count Lev Tolstoy wrote
keen misery finds evermore
imaginative ways to slake
its need for tender prey.

From long-sought rest
comes little motivation;
in sleepless dread
expressive senses twitch.

Mild content dulls,
whereas frustration whets
the creative edge
that craves delight.

In the house of mourning
fundamental joys
yield fresh abundance
sorrow cannot hold in check.

The Laughing Calvinist

Far from the grim image of pursed-lipped Puritans
promulgated by their own late-blooming hysteria
and Hawthorne (now as far from us as he from them),
staunch catechists I've known are among
the wittiest and most jovial companions,
cracking wise about predestination
and prone to audacious literary jokes.
Their puns are the worst—proof
of fundamental good nature; the more
groan-worthy, the better,
as all merry-hearted patriarchs know.

Poetry

It shoulders my apartment doorbell well after dark,
staggers through the vestibule, and drops sobbing on my sofa,
bewailing the callousness and perfidy of ex-lovers and current
    coworkers.

I was just about to go to bed.
Fresh from the shower, in clean jammies,
unguents smoothed over my hands and face to keep wrinkles from
    entrenching overnight.
And suddenly I am thrust into a maelstrom of emotion, passion,
    and complaint.

I proffer a selection of herbal teas and wait for the kettle's pained
    scream
to drown out the moans and mutterings from the couch.
Hot porcelain at my elbow,
I hope my prostrate guest says something coherent.
Sometimes I hear wild tales,
sometimes a short pastoral,
at other moments only curses and colors.

There are months it doesn't visit,
and weeks when it comes calling every day,
when I meet it on the street even in broad daylight,
or it interrupts a class, to everyone's chagrin,
times when we stay up past midnight discussing every subject
    under the moon.

I don't know how long we can stay friends.
Are we, even?
Such irregular co-dependency is complicated.

Smelly Feat

Inspiration wagged its eager tail
and ran off into the trees,
whence it soon emerged,
dragging mortal fragments
of some unidentifiable creature
stinking and buzzing with flies.
It rolled gleefully in the mess
and then ran up to me,
proud of its accomplishment.

Spirit

A bar can be a good place to pray.
Nobody minds you mumbling into your cocktail.
It's too loud for private chats to be overheard.
You can cry to Christ about the state of the world,
rail against its war-torn edges,
contemplate eternity across the salted rim,
through the double barrel of the opaque stir straw,
and other patrons and the staff will simply think
your soulfulness comes from excess spirits.
You can sip and simmer secretly in mindful love,
consider the incarcerated and the displaced,
scroll through oppression and messages,
plan how to spend your small social capital fighting evil,
fumble rhymes (so many hymns set to drinking tunes!),
and ask the Almighty for the otherwise impossible.
Be still in the chaotic dark, assured of *aqua vit*
gratis, inexhaustible.

Words II

At Sunday open mics
he records sharp words
to general applause.
On dusty weekday curbs
he pinches penned cardboard
and squints desperation
beside the asphalt roar
of soundproofed vehicles.

Publisher's Lunch

A leaf from her salad fluttered to the floor.
"I'm being defenestrated," she yelped.
"Defoliated," her colleague corrected,
picking up and tossing the errant spinach out the window.
"Not deflowered?" asked their admin
as they buried their nose in their new bouquet
and waggled their eyebrows at the delivery guy,
who looked around in confusion. "What the fu—?"
"That's the idea!" the admin said. "But we're spoken for."
"I speak for the trees," said the salad-eater.
"Naked or otherwise," agreed her colleague.
The delivery guy left, muttering about nuts.

Contemplating Autobiography

There was nothing presently worthwhile
in her old correspondence,
no unconscious novel composed
over several years of college emails.
Dried corsage flowers from a forgotten dance,
the enthusiasm and despair there was without context,
youthful mementoes fallen apart,
inconsequential activities and long-lost contacts,
and the needless stress of academic classes
whose information had been irrelevant decades since.
I am not like that person anymore, she realized.
Any tale salvaged from those outdated files
must needs be framed of new timber,
and the cutting might not be worth
either deaths of trees or loss of time.

Restless Spirit

Through a glass I look deep
beyond the hair and marrow,
to what makes people bleed.
Then my thoughts run
unfettered by social mores
and my forehead burns
with feverish ideas.
This also happens when I am
estranged from sleep—
he trails doting fingertips
over others' eyelids
while he shuns my bed.
So I dream awake
of adulterous possibilities
fueled by fatigue and wine.

Insomnia

My stomach warm with bread,
milk, honey, chamomile,
I lie down at midnight.

Three hours thence I stare
dry-eyed into the black
air beyond the bedclothes.

I take stock countless times;
stay innocent of light;
grimly muffle noises;

Relax each tight fiber;
imagine nothingness;
despair in wild prayer.

Yet rest scrambles away,
its claws tearing my plans,
puncturing my dreams.

Last, I watch time fluoresce,
reject my need for sleep—
helpless in looming dawn.

To Rest

You'd think sleeping meds
these days would have their own fragrant style.
"I'll have the Vanilla Swirl, please."
"Double Dutch Chocolate has wonderful dreams."
"Cotton Candy and Cream Cheese soothe the anxious soul."
I want that thick milk in my veins
that slid me into sudden oblivion
before my annual colonoscopy—
unawareness achieved with one push of the needle—
only without the previous purging and the injection.
It could be perfectly catered (aroma, depth, duration),
with occasional open-ended no-time-limit naps
varying from a few hours to a day-and-a-half;
from a single scoop to an over-filled, dripping waffle cone.
But maybe we insomniacs are would-be Van Winkles
wisely deprived of relaxation by night-owl nature.
The ability to choose sweet slumber might stop time for us,
while the rest of the vegetable world would roll blandly on,
forgetting our existence.

Good Sleep

I float softly
in happy dreams
as a silver balloon
trailing its string
across a drafty room
or an open field

Limp and content
within strollers' easy reach
cupping corners
subsiding into branches
shining in the sun

Theological Tanka

Each Bible hero—
people who became great saints
in the end of ends—
felt tangibles stripped away
in the maturing process.

Academy

My younger students are squirrels
with the attention span of gnats,
always twittering among themselves
and borne along by rushes of emotion,
only circumstantially attracted to the subject
I am contracted to teach them.
My snide remarks on their inability to concentrate
loft harmlessly over their flighty little heads,
while simple slights from classmates
reduce them to quick-welling tears
which I must soothe with careful sympathy
and stern warnings that all should practice kindness.

ESOL

She craved the haze two glasses granted
after five days' wrangling high-pitched pupils
through basic elements of a foreign language.

Friday nights she sipped from a juice-filled tumbler
and sighed at intractable communication problems
as her tongue thickened with each mouthful of quiet.

Pencils

Those cupped on my desk
once dropped in headlong rushes for the door
and remained unclaimed thereafter.
Some are embossed with advertising,
others printed in cartoons.
Most are sharpened short and wanting their erasers.

(The larger independent rubber bits
I've found are in another jar.)

They wait for those who come without
tools to take daily notes
or to scribble answers on my biweekly tests.

The abandoned supply the unprepared.

Junior High

I want to pinch her little head off,
like a bad sprout on a tomato plant.
How can she toss her hair,
roll her eyes like that
and remain upright? Perhaps
she's realizing her peak at 14?
Fine. I shouldn't like to interrupt
that fleeting sense of superior worth,
but her attitude is nigh intolerable.
If I can just maintain my cool in class
and ensure she learns enough to pass,
on some far distant day she could
become a decent anthropoid.

Respite

What affords relief to everyday tedium?
Flights of non-criminal whimsy
that astound children or coworkers:
when you didn't give a piece of your mind
and abruptly did a little dance
in the middle of the room.

Seogwipo Weekday, 3 PM

Aromas from kitchens and covert cigarettes
waft among parked cars and idle dogs.
A pair of stained men clutch green glass bottles
under a leafless tree.
A dame in odd florals diligently stretches,
while sparrows peck a playground's plastic soccer pitch.
Then, at the echoes of a single tone,
a flood of schoolchildren pours around the corner.

Garden Stitchery

I wish the weeds in my front yard
were sewn like buttons on a card,
not tangled with the wrong side out,
their surplus roots so long and stout
it's nigh impossible to rip
them from their deeply woven grip.
Tares are resilient and rough—
those plants we want are not so tough:
their fibers weak, they quickly wilt,
whereas the hardy burrs still quilt
our cherished flowerbeds and lawn.
The gardener must arise at dawn,
to salvage ragged pavement lines,
sow salts to ward off growing vines.
A dyed fool slattern I may seem,
my grand design a silly dream—
while I tear out a pattern patch
my work looks like a wrestling match.
All stained with soil from hat to toe,
I trim the hedge, apply my hoe,
bind up the refuse with a cord,
well-gloved, face needle thorns ungored,
redressing now the natural waste—
cute mushrooms slash to suit my taste.

Volcano

Beneath us is consuming fire.

The infected earth abruptly shakes and coughs.
Split roads smoke.

Frantic residents grab documents, pictures, pets, and run.
Their tire marks on sun-faded asphalt
are soon swallowed by crawling lava.

Ravenous photographers ignore officials
to angle for the perfect shot
of molten rock geysers,
orange-silhouetted palm trees,
and sweat-bathed refugees.

A rainforest melts to ash.

Downstream, a torrent of scarlet stone
explodes against the boiling cold ocean.

Relics vanish under new land—
hard, grey, pinched, bubbled,
expectant.

Fissures

Asphalt's winter flaws
accumulate spring's leavings:
pollen, bruised petals.

Deep Winter, 2020, Korea

It was colder than a Kodiak gold miner's bum.
We wind-nipped walkers wept into our masks,
scarfs bound tight around our necks and chins,
hands shoved deep into last year's stale crumbs,
and shoulders hunched protectively towards our naked ears
(red and ringing in the abrupt chill).
At sundown, when dead leaves tap-tapped
uncertainly on the hypothermic asphalt,
shedding fusty odors when crushed underfoot,
we sought warm floors, hot wine, and sizzling romance,
able to savor the last only in sterile electronic form.

South/North, Winter 2025

Where the road curves, a solid matte-black motorcycle helmet
perches ominously atop a heavy wooden cross.
Barren fire ant hills, child-drawn Golgothas
sit spaced throughout the evergreen grass.
Kissing trees, bare but for balls of mistletoe,
and pines split in half by an autumn hurricane
stand helplessly behind enormous piles of grey-brown logs.

Snow lies on the smooth shoulders and arms of the beeches,
while the torn skin of the river birches reaches to the sky.
Well-wrapped rosy children shriek with joy,
sliding down a hill between two neighboring houses.
Even in this city-close settlement, there are hoofprints
of deer and soft tracks of foxes running through the white drifts:
simple tales of wild activity in the stillness of the night.

Advent Sweets

Warm chocolate in wintertime
keeps the cold at mitten ends
and curves chilled cheeks
with whipped-cream smiles.

Three eastern kings,
cinnamon, ginger, and cloves,
spice cakes and cookies
cut out in sugar-glittered stars.

Christmas peppermints
redden lips moist from
mistletoe kisses until
pulses race and eyes sparkle.

Jolly

Wretched hostages, netted Christmas trees'
heads hang over the tailgate,
hair swaying in the wind
while the people in the cab laugh and joke,
driving home to dress the bodies.

Wanderer's Dilemma

Leaning over a guardrail
late one winter evening,
heaving her carsick guts
into the abyss,
the traveler wondered
whether adventure
were as good for the soul
as it was unkind
to the digestive system.

Tampa Tanka

A tight flock of pink
flamingoes walks together,
their webbed feet raindrops
splashing active red puddles
on grassy Florida sand.

Urban Late Summer

AC compressors blow hot drafts
across steaming motorways
where crushed creatures swell and fester.
Weeds reek and snarled cables sag overhead.
Stickiness coats sunburnt necks,
chafing elbows, armpits, thighs.
Nighttime smog screens the moon
while artificial light bleaches
leashed humans dragged by panting dogs,
and insects chuckle derisively from the dark.

Storm Coming

Afternoon arrives grey, ominous.
Temperamental winds
yank open umbrellas.
Unbalanced last-minute pedestrians
dodge heaps of mildewed boards
from a gutted restaurant.

The cyclone locks residents in
dry, double-paned rooms
to wash dishes, smooth wrinkled clothes,
and complete other long-ignored domestic chores,
or to sleep drowned in wind-noise
until blue skies appear.

Monsoon Season

Hand outstretched to raindrops,
a boy in a marigold shirt
stands under a sagging restaurant awning.
He smiles at each splash,
the silver of a cloudy summer day.

Fall

shadows and sunlight
sift wind-borne
yellow leaves

autumn drifts flutter
from branches arched
above tall rock walls

roots knotted on
chiseled heights
guard the stream

trickling from
warm stepping stones
to deep cool baths

where great boulders
grow blue-green
and unperturbed

Autumn Walk

The fallen leaves scatter like chickens.
A squadron of ducks float on the river,
silently paddling upstream,
hunting among the rocks and
rippling reflections of late-afternoon sunshine.
A white crane steps among the reeds along the bank
and a large grey crane stands proudly on a stone in the center of the stream.
Cameras do not understand up or down, heat or cold.
They record angles, not feelings,
so my amateur attempts to pixelate
the pleasure of my surroundings
yields unpretty birds.

Fall/Winter

At lingerie shops, mannequins favor flannel over lace.
Steam rises from Americanos in thick indolent curls
while, beyond the glass, snow flurries
melt instantly on rooftops and sidewalks,
accumulating on silent air conditioning units.

Bodega

Melancholy cat
beside a watermelon
observing olives.

Economy Class

In aluminum-skinned tubes
airless hours pass under uniformed eyes.
A dim calm contradicts the engines' devouring roar
as fares packed like paraboloid potato chips
wait for the ritual extinguishing of signs.
Rather than betray their fellows to leverage relief,
the resolute endure upright,
counting flight time till release.

Eve

When the knife slipped,
juice dripped
from the split flesh
onto the wooden board.

She'd cleft the whorl
into competing hemispheres,
another in her catalog
of self-inflicted scars.

Magdalene

We want love for who we are
but blindly shove aside that sober dream
for breathless nights' requited lust
with those who vanish in the sun,
calls unanswered and texts unread.

Belated questions of disease
supersede our acquired indifference.
Each abortion fragments the self.
Still, we hope for someone
undaunted by our layered scars.

At Sunday's lonely daybreak,
when we sit wracked with helpless tears,
One offers a torn, earth-stained hand
and calls us quietly by name.

Missing

I doubt the testimony of the neighbor
who said he was 70% sure a carcass
glimpsed three days ago was Marmalade.
I think he was just weary of my friend's
relentless searches for her beloved.
When we went to look at the spot,
there was nothing but a few feathers—
remnants of an unfortunate bird
who'd stopped to inspect the dead—
and desiccated matter pounded
into asphalt cracks by speeding traffic.
It could have been fur or fowl,
but past foul and past recognition
on any level other than the molecular.
My friend blames herself. I say
country cats have their own will;
for a decade almost, he and his fellows
had been wandering fields and hedges.
That he vanished moving day
is no blot on her affectionate character.
The busy road is far, and he may yet be
on a quest of which we know nothing.
But she is inconsolable.

Ocean Tanka

Dying jellyfish
upended, vulnerable,
floating on the tide,
their delicate structure clear
images of galaxies.

Showoffs

Roosters disturb me, those sun-trumpeters.
Suspicion stares from their round eyes,
beaks pursed in spinsterish disapproval
while their necks jerk spasmodically,
wattles trembling like flaccid scrotal sacs.
They constantly strut, shout and fight
to prove their masculine credentials.
Teiresias would laugh to see this ritual display.
I'm told their flesh tends toward the stringy,
but I'd make do with a good tzatziki sauce.

Fashion Show

By training visibly dissatisfied,
tall straws stalk unmarked paths
in peculiar handcrafts exaggerated
to cover or reveal in ways
only empresses can afford.
Off-stage, relieved mannequins
shed their weird skins, wipe away paint,
and cheerfully don loose sweats
no one films but all comfort-envy.

Irish Seahorses

At the mouth of the river
young bareback racers
thunder beneath jagged bluffs.
The sandy pace taxes
fathers' patience
and worries mothers—
both yelling, "Hold on!"
and "Faster, just a bit!"
Children urge their mounts
with shrill cries soon
lost in the fierce wind.

Medieval Calligraphy

Childless ascetics
inscribed hours
in ebony
and leaf gold,
illuminating prose
with the wonder
and color of
the divine garden,
idly adding adolescent doodles:
absurd figures quarrelling
and farting in the margins.

Cyclist

Atop a sleek frame with skinny pork-tint tires,
a knife-edged seat leans against the café wall.

Its owner, the trim pony-tailed barista, recalls an episode from
his brief New York boyhood—

"Someone gave us a used single-speed with wobbly training
    wheels.
The rubber handgrips had pink ribbons on the ends.

One day, this huge, brawny guy, his knees out sideways,
peddled off toward the sunrise on my 'girly' bike.

The last I saw of it as he disappeared around the corner
were the streamers fluttering in the morning frost."

Deserving

There absolutely ought to be
a medal for humility.
I would win it in a flash
of self-denial: touch greasy ash
to my forehead, wear a gown
in tatters and a beatific frown.

Admire my look of studied virtue!
no hair shirt for me—they'll hurt you
where your suffering's unseen.
What good is there in being sore
when no one knows or can adore
your saintliness routine?

Covid

The Fates poked a twig into humanity's ant-pile,
stirred it to watch us frantically run, collecting sand,
and fly to spittle-build our dislodged hornets' nests.
Our fat, slow monarchs reacted variously,
workers' lives indelibly disrupted,
sacrificing their one dying sting
on behalf of an ignorant hive.

2022

My secret exercise was worthless.

In the privacy of my bedroom,
I tried to channel all the enthusiasm
of an eighteenth-century satin-suited snuff-taker,
of a corncob-smoking country grandma
hawking phlegm into a coffee-can spittoon.

For more than two years, I had carefully eschewed
any solid up-with-the-guts into-the-gutters waistband-busters.
But without a shocked audience, I couldn't muster
the indecent strength to break the long-observed taboo.

2020s

New years wailing disconsolately
for the comfort of the womb
kick hourglasses from tables
and crawl out broken windows
to drop headfirst onto concrete walks
where mastiffs growl at delivery people
and crooks curse poverty with greater want.

Fear

Fear is a migraine,
throbbing nausea inside
bending the furniture,
making light unbearable.

Fear enervates and stabs,
willing you to swallow poison
to achieve painlessness
and peace of mind.

Castration/Consumption

For two millennia, Europeans gelded choirboys and cockerels
before adolescence ruined their voices and added needless
　　plumage;
domestic consumers desired the heavy breasts of mature capons,
the massive sopranos of mutilated men.
Today's Westerners still discount mass sterilizations
that undergird our appetite for cheap imported goods.

Philosophical

What is the context
which prompts someone to belt out
"Grimy Gopher Guts"?

Georgia

Gravel peppers your pollen-filmed windshield
on Peachtree-wormed compound interstates
decorated by crossing failures and lost furniture.
Giant billboards shout of gun and bridal shows, last stops,
churches, lawyers, budget car repair, and surgeons.
Freight trains rumble through nighttime zombie towns
and long daylit trucks of tapered pine logs
snort and swing wide around two-laned corners.
Below the mountains, dashboards bake in the shade
at flat sand beaches or rolling pick-your-own farms,
while you'll be abruptly deep-frozen indoors
(always carry a sweater in your purse in August!).
We are the New South—sprawling, smiling, soft-drawling
kitchen saints who'll find, save, and feed your soul
off deer-rich swamp-spotted farmland marked "posted."
Our scars and beauties are held equally sacred.
Short generations removed from segregation,
we mix cotton, hip-hop, peanuts, and Hollywood.

Dixie Barista

Hon, take a look over yonder.
That guy—just out of the blue car.
Well, I may be old enough to be his grandma,
but this girl still has eyes.
Holy cow. He's a fine-looking young man.

Good morning, sir.
How can I help you?
Latte? Small or large?
That'll be five seventy-eight.

Where you from?
Korea. North or South?
Hah! I knew you weren't some damn Yankee.
Your Mama and Daddy and God together
should be proud of what they created.

Do you like chocolate? Yes?
Well, here's a cookie on the house.
Just for brightening up my day.
You have a good one, hear?

A Southern Psalm

Thou anointest my cornbread with honey.
My sweet iced tea overflows.
Though there may be tough rows to hoe,
Goodness, grace, and mercy
shall stop by in all weathers of my life,
and I will rest and rock gently
on the Almighty's screened-in porch forever.

Antique Music

A whiskery insect skitters among
broken hymnals and tattered sheet music.
A row of stops faced in gothic type beams
from wood cracked into fine elephant hide.
Pairs of corn husk and sleek Asian dolls lean
towards a player rocking on the stool.
The machine wheezes as she pedals
resolutely on worn Persian carpet,
determined to milk its broken bellows.
Her fingers press the ivory teeth—
one stained by a midcentury cigarette burn—
and their voices quaver with memories.

Saving and Spending

As a child I watched my grandmama
carefully paint half-open lips
with a slender sable brush,
dabbing cream from a mostly empty tube.
This doodlebug economy carried over from her youth
of handsewn floral flour sack dresses
modeled on pictures from Sears & Roebuck catalogs.
Hands shaking, she still smooths torn foil flat
and wipes it down to cover scraps
from huge meals she cooks—Thanksgiving every day—
her lifetime savings lavished all on others.

Fungus Haiku

I am a mushroom,
sitting in the silent dark,
growing soft and round.

Gym Notice

To the testosterone-addled monster
who broke my workout rhythm,
rudely asserting his moment at the weight bench
was more vital than my awkward calisthenics:
Your meaty arms aren't strong enough
to counteract the effect of your BCGs,
Mister Wrist Wraps.

Size of Resignation

I remember what it was to be muscular.
Now my skin texture resembles
a sack of frozen peas.
Basically a pudding on legs,
I should refine my type—
no more underdone tapioca
when I could be crème brûlée!

Ode to 'The Change'

You give me unprecedented courage,
but have me gulp predawn javas
to achieve minimal coherence,
and sip chamomile to doze
fitfully past midnight.
Your abrupt fluxes
demand winter tanks
and summer parkas.
You flatten my posterior,
yet inflate my waist;
first, I am a rung-out mop,
then an over-stuffed goose.
Altogether, though, are you so bad?
I've relinquished lunar misery
and have grown neither horns nor hooves.

Boobs Haiku

Let those bold bosoms
do what they will: bounce, jiggle,
just sag with relief.

Unmatched

She sits mute, aching to be clever.
A ball lodges behind her belly button,
a fist-sized lump of longing to explode witticisms.
She admires those who send one salvo after another flying,
lobs and volleys returned with gusto,
a game of verbal tennis over the dinner table.
She can listen and laugh, an appreciative spectator.
But as with wielding a physical racket,
it would be pure chance were her own serve to connect,
less likelihood of its crossing the net at any speed
to land in-bounds, and none at all
of its initiating even the shortest series of returns.
Well, we can't all be the Williams sisters of one-liners.

Beverages

Graceful curls of steam
from fresh coffee cups
flip feline tails
under the noses
of early risers.

The icy lips
of late-night bottles
kiss openmouthed,
pouring welcome drafts
down dog-tired throats.

Cold

Mentally, I'm gelatin.
Germs have reduced my body
to a semi-conscious amoeba.
I feel like I'm dog-paddling
through tepid, viscous fluid.
A tight band twists
between my eardrums,
muting their beat,
and my tongue, too, is mostly inert—
the only things I can taste are salt,
apathy, and a little sweetness.
On such occasions, I thank God
for decongestants, sick days, and bed.

Holiday Solitude

The barman perches on an iron stool,
sipping iced tea,
silently amused at texts.

The occasional mosquito pricks my fingers—
sugar-jittery from hot chocolate and Kahlua,
unseasonable sweets in the stifling twilight.

The wine bar window-wall
opens to a cobblestone street.
Flies form a lazy tornado midair.

I watch pairs and groups of tourists
disappear up or down the hill,
out of sync with the jazz inside.

The barman lights small candles at the empty tables
and I order a belated stem of house red
rather than return to my lonely hotel room.

Jungang Rotary on Buddha's Birthday

At midnight, the prayer wheel of city streets
revolving the lantern-lit roundabout slows and stills,
in its center glows a bell, a large pale jellyfish.
Tomcats battle beneath sidewalk-parked cars.
Scores of stoplights blink against the wind.
Discarded shopping bags slide and shuffle,
and motorbikes growl, their masked riders
returning from deliveries to hungry apartments.
Guttural clunks echo as taxis roll over sewer lids
embossed "Made in Korea" in Latin type.
Convenience store doors squeak and chime
when students in pajamas and soft sandals
step out, arms filled with sweet, salty snacks.
Above them, a bronze god flexes on a banner,
his muscle-bound navel resembling an infected cyst.
Parka-clad foreigners turn, staring at their phones,
waiting for an elusive signal to direct their paths.
The calm firmament arches over all, declaring glories
unheeded by bulging bellies and absent minds.

Tiger Food

A Christmas tree ziggurat
of empty soju bottles
stands outside the restaurant
whose round steel tables miss
their central charcoal burners.
The hungry crowds grilling *samgyeopsal**
or seasoned beef will assemble after dark.
From the stall next door, eyebrow-curling chili pepper
wafts off a crimson pan of *ddeokbokki*
(insipid rice-paste logs submerged in fiery sauce)—
schoolchildren's favorite snack,
eaten with toothpicks out of paper cups.
The South Korean tiger proves
its fierceness in consumption
of flames and fumes.

samgyeopsal—thick bacon triple-striped with fat

Observance, 2022

Today is my birthday.
I ordered my own cake—
blatantly against Korean tradition,
but I will have a delicious treat
from a small shop that makes them on-site,
rather than some chain's concoction
with a chemical aftertaste.
Someone recently fell
into an industrial mixer at the latter's factory.
The company sent bread
from the same facility to her funeral.
Huge scandal, but as accidents go
hereabouts, not the worst.
Blame-shifting for lives lost
in the Itaewon crowd-crush continues.
"Adults" aren't taking responsibility
for not preventing the Halloween disaster
wherein people who hadn't celebrated
half as many birthdays as I
died in masked revelry.

Weekdays

shrill alarms chase
peaceful sleep panicked
to the breakfast table
and thence out the door
to school and the office
where we sit like rocks
among shoreward ripples
and then gulp lunch only
to starve until late supper
after assorted afternoon
and evening meetings
belatedly release us
stumbling across curbs
to collapse on the sofa
for shows and snacks
then melt in showers
and fall back into bed

Conspiracy Theorists

Armpit literature, screenshot:
They're keeping secrets from you . . .
Here's the real story, the original text—
just read this, unwashed masses,
consult the boil at your chest-high beltline
as the void stares into your soul and cabals
control the communication means by which we share
our stories of international machinations
in single-minded efforts to draw more views.
Ad revenues pile up as we beat the capitalist horse
until it dies in accordance with our prognostications,
but not before your credulity has financed
unaccountable luxuries.

Treasure

Some stones were missing,
but the tiara was remarkably intact,
wearable once the sand was rinsed off.
Where had it come from?
A beach wedding? A fashion shoot?
Or an ocean kingdom where seawomen
sparkle in gems and iridescent scales,
their veil-like fins undulating
with currents miles beneath the waves?

Be Nimble

Flexibility
and speed will take you beyond
expectations, man.

Search Fail

In the throes of fruitless job hunting, he thought,
Perhaps I could become a body collector.
From a childhood terrified of Egyptian mummy photos
to being unaffected by parlor-prepared corpses,
had he come to the point where he could manage
the rotting remnants of those outside his acquaintance?
The dead are dead. It does need to be done.
If he were so unfortunate as to perish beyond the limits
of banal urban existence, he would hope
someone would find his emerging bones and secure them.
However, brief inquiry revealed a severe, distinctive odor—
People frequently get nauseated catching just a whiff—
one allegedly hard to expunge, to the point
the living reeked thereafter of decomposition.
Even the thought of rotting tomatoes made him gag.
. . . maybe this is one job I shouldn't consider.

Player

Don't bet on cheating him to win.

Unkindly crippled, cut away,
bereft of rank and active roles:
whatever fate you draw will lose
to his house full of kings and knaves.

The elder in the striped suit
who fans and calls the glossy cards
slips aces down from his silk cuffs.
His heartless hand declares you blind
and in turn runs out the clock.

He then discards a shuffling pile
of fallen acorns, dry blown leaves
which widows sweep and set alight.

Mortal Dread

He became increasingly terrified
of his own frame:
the skull that weighed on his pillow,
hidden behind hair and skin;
the fleshed phalanges
reaching toward his face;
the cavities trapping his eyeballs—
orbs which vanished unaccountably into
a grinning menace on cranial x-rays.
Death always lurked just out of sight,
cracking his joints and threatening
to make his mobile corpse decay
faster than it already was.

Sacrifices

Bloodthirsty, we spit puce clots from raw throats,
trapped flies knocking against windows, seeking
to escape the space between glass and screen.
At birth, our mothers writhe as we emerge,
cream-slicked and wailing, into unsought light.
We weep for joy under white wedding tents,
and through adulthood and at the last, we
fight the ropes drawing us toward silence,
to rot in deep maggot-breeding wombs.
Or is our clawing at the gentle hands
that would rescue us from that yawning pit—
a dead panic that rends help's side and brow
and willfully pulls hope into the dark?

Wrinkles

youth's fabric creased by middle-aged
ruts of habit and circumstance
tear trails and laugh lines
powerfully telegraphing character
nesting memories
and long-flown ambitions

Recompense

I once criticized those
who spent pounds of cash
on dubious beauty remedies.
Now I nightly drip serum
derived of crushed flowers,
chopped leaves,
and disemboweled fruits
from a glass pipette
onto my flaccid cheeks
in hope that the youth
it purports to restore
blooms in direct proportion
to its dearness.

Veteran

The pinched man with grey threads
arching over his sun-splotched scalp
was once a thick-thatched boy—

plump-cheeked with a mischievous grin,
eating sweets outside school,
who shied away from glancing girls.

Unfiltered conscript smokes and
decades of civilian social drinks
have unspooled and sapped him.

If pried from that wizened core,
would his heart seed yield
fresh or embittered fruit?

Sideswipe

Judge the face and judge the figure;
crossing later in the street,
left or right, you mean to give her
business manners when you meet.

Fresh-tinted lips force too-bright smiles
dead eyes do not reflect.
In empty words on full profiles
egotism reigns unchecked.

Haunted

Sometimes she catches a glimpse of it
darting beneath a dirty dish on the counter,
subsiding into a long-unvacuumed corner,
or drifting across the surface of her eyeball.
More than once, she thought it rang the bell
(those might have been echoes from next door).
Her wards against its definitive appearance
include bug spray, rags, saline, and earplugs.
Alas, mortality is not so easily deterred.

Before, Then, After

Thirsty plants and insects crawl
over the sill of the fractured window.

Suddenly, spring arrives,
floods of fresh-decanted passion.

Withered weeds adorn the table
behind the crooked knob of the old door.

February 13, 2021

Valentine's eve saw him in tears.
Another Lunar Year had dawned.
He did not weep for the white ox,
but for a sandwich-cookie cow
with a turgid udder lowing and
waiting in a deserted barnyard.
He anticipated hot romance
that never came. However,
he was able to console himself
with a bar of dark chocolate
and a cold glass of oat milk.

Questions

Did you end up like your dad?

Spending evenings
staring blankly at a television,
unspeaking at dinner,
blending into an old recliner,
wrinkled work shirt merged
with sallow floral velvet?

His was not satisfied silence,
but brute muteness, animal fatigue,
too abused and disabused of hope
to voice any complaint.

You were so earnest,
struggling against the current,
directly confronting hardships
I had only known from dystopian novels,
that I (until then) would not quite allow
existed so close by.

Diligently you had pulled yourself up,
over the rim of that childhood pit,
into possibilities and experiences
beyond your family's understanding.

I still admire your strength.

You bore marks. Small as they were,
their worth grew as I looked at your
kind, bland mother and sagging father—
and painfully recognized our differences.

How my family, for all its flaws,
didn't reek of resignation.
How we were relatively spendthrift,
simply could afford nice things;
I had never had to do without
to the bone-scraping extent you knew.

Terrified of penury, of the barefoot grit
which brought you and yours
to bare-walled middle-class subsistence,
a painful veneer of solvency,
I wrote that letter. Was I weak?

A quarter century on, have you
joined your father in that dim corner?

Or does he remain there only in my heart
as a poignant symbol of loss?

Ideal

You are precisely what I hoped for
down to the printed letter,
as if some devil read
my unspoken list and advertised,
or crafted dreams into hot flesh
and cold blood.
Of course, as with all underworld
designs, there is one crucial missing
element that demands
a self-destructive sacrifice,
a great divorce
of heavenly satisfaction
from lustful mortality.

Outdated

Cicadas emit a loud electrostatic buzz,
desperately dialing up coupling sites
at the end of their short summer lives.

Once

Just once, before I lose all vestiges
of romantic inclination, could I be desirable?
Someone around whom a lover wraps his arms,
whose shoulders, cheeks, neck
irresistibly draw his eyes and lips?
I am an off-key singer; my figure is operatic.
I neither cook nor drink beer,
yet I look to be the goodwife of ales and hearty meals,
unencumbered bosoms and ribald tongue
who roundly beckons Shakespearean rogues.
Still, I am unnoticed within the dim corner
where I quietly ink repressed desire.

Medusa

Her hair immortal
coiled in hissing knots, she eyed
statuesque young men
with suspicion born
of wisdom's censure.

Twilight

Woodsmoke trickles from
a waterside bar's chimney—
ideal autumn smell.
Streetlights in shady places
begin to turn on automatically,
and the eastern horizon sublimes into the sky.
A chained dog barks and growls from atop its plastic house,
its beady eyes fluorescent in the failing light.
The remaining leaves on the trees shuffle sleepily,
the sea starts to whisper, "Shhh, shhh . . .,"
and the birds tell each other bedtime stories.
The passage of a jet far overhead
prompts us to hold hands.

Mature Chemistry

A growing pill pile rests
in the cervical depression
on my third pillow—
not just the handful
an aging Seuss forecast
to be bolted at bedtime,
but an assortment of colors
and embossed shapes culled from
absent sanity and digestion,
all assembled to dull unwanted
sensitivities and maintain
those that threaten to disappear.
Tonight I swallow what
tomorrow will purge.

Visit

This room has a close-up view
of another high-rise window
where creaky pigeons preen
and push sunshine off the ledge.

Nighttime is fluorescent glow.

Old acquaintances drop in
to squeeze my withered hands
in reinforcement of their charity
and lie, *You look good.*

Intent on our respective lives,
we rarely got together.

Now, too soon—
You're getting tired.
It's time we left.
I have to go make dinner.

Reclaimed

Rainbows of makeup pencils
in unlabeled glass jars
clutter the top of the chest
she discovered in a local rubbish pile.
Its shiny black corners are chipped,
and some of the pearlescent birds
are missing feet and feathers,
but in the elegance of the old piece
there is enduring beauty.

Undetermined

She's not really in a rush to meet life's milestones,
still tripping over her own feet, milling around.
Her peers are on the cusp of welcoming grandchildren,
and she's had only her first kiss, one boyfriend.
Most are in the middle of mortgages,
and she's yet to decide on a country to take root in,
much less a piece of property she'd like to buy.
Eventually, the latter will be decided for her—
She'll have a patch of ground that is forever hers.
But of course, if she's cremated, she'll continue to wander,
not settled enough even in death to push up a daisy.

Late Love

Youth had long since left off blushing
when each fell suddenly, entirely
head-over-heels for the other.
His sallow complexion
and her wrinkled face
lit up from the inside.
Neither might have been beautiful,
but shared affection unburdened them,
wreathed their faces with smiles,
and replaced featureless existence
with holiday color and festivity.
Observant untried romantics,
once over the initial shock
at this autumn miracle,
absolutely envied them.

About the Author

Born in Texas and raised in the Central Savannah River Area (CSRA) of Georgia, USA, Christina E. Petrides lived and worked on Jeju Island, Republic of Korea, 2017–2023, where she began writing poetry. Christina's first poetry collection was *On Unfirm Terrain* (Kelsay Books, 2022); *The Laughing Calvinist* is her second collection. Many of the pieces in each collection were first published in periodicals around the world.

Christina is the author of multiple children's books: *Blueberry Man* (2020); *The Refrigerator Ghost* (2022); *Tea Cakes, Quilts, and Sonshine* (2022); *Mr. Fisher's Whiskers* (2024); and *My Batty Aunt Betty* (2025). Additionally, Christina served as the primary translator of Maria Shelyakhovskaya's *Being Grounded in Love: A History of One Russian Family, 1872–1981* (2023).

Website:
www.christinaepetrides.com

Substack:
@christinaepetrides

www.ingramcontent.com/pod-product-compliance
Lightning Source LLC
Chambersburg PA
CBHW072200160426
43197CB00012B/2471